Valentine's Day Magic

Valentine's Day Magic

Matthew Petchinsky

Valentine's Day Magic: A Guide to Romantic Rituals
By: Matthew Petchinsky

Introduction: Infusing Love and Intention into Valentine's Day

Valentine's Day has long been celebrated as a day of love, romance, and heartfelt gestures. However, beneath the commercial sheen of roses, chocolates, and lavish dinners lies an opportunity to create deeper, more meaningful connections by weaving love and intention into the fabric of this special day. In *Valentine's Day Magic: A Guide to Romantic Rituals*, we invite you to go beyond the surface-level expressions of affection and embrace the profound, transformative power of love rituals.

This guide is not merely about romance in its traditional sense; it's about cultivating an enduring connection to the energy of love in all its forms—romantic, self-love, and universal compassion. Through carefully crafted rituals, meditations, and acts of intention, you'll learn how to harness the magic of Valentine's Day to create moments of lasting beauty, joy, and connection.

The Spirit of Valentine's Day

At its core, Valentine's Day is a celebration of connection, a day to honor the bonds we share with those we love. This tradition, steeped in history and lore, finds its roots in ancient Roman festivals, the romanticism of medieval courtly love, and the mystical energy associated with Saint Valentine himself. While the day has evolved over centuries, its essence remains the same: to cherish and celebrate the relationships that enrich our lives.

But love is more than just an emotion; it is an energy that permeates everything we do. It's the force that inspires creativity, fuels compassion, and sparks the joy of simply being present with another. By approaching Valentine's Day with mindful intention, we can transform it from a commercial holiday into a sacred celebration of this powerful energy.

Why Rituals Matter

Rituals have always been a vital part of human culture, serving as tools to focus our energy, clarify our intentions, and connect us with something greater than ourselves. Whether lighting a candle for someone we care about or sharing a meal imbued with gratitude, these seemingly small acts can be profoundly transformative when performed with mindfulness and purpose.

In this guide, you'll discover rituals that go beyond the ordinary. Each one is designed to bring magic into your Valentine's Day, turning simple gestures into moments of enchantment. These rituals will help you cultivate an atmosphere of love, not just for your partner but for yourself and the world around you.

What You'll Find in This Book

Valentine's Day Magic: A Guide to Romantic Rituals is a treasure trove of ideas and practices to help you infuse love and intention into this special day. Whether you're celebrating with a partner, a group of loved ones, or by yourself, there's something here for everyone. Here's a glimpse of what lies ahead:

- **Romantic Rituals for Two**: Explore rituals that deepen connection and intimacy with your partner, from shared love spells to enchanted bath rituals.
- **Self-Love Practices**: Embrace the magic of self-love through affirmations, journaling, and indulgent self-care rituals.
- **Creative Celebrations**: Discover unique ways to celebrate love with friends, family, or your community, including group meditations and collaborative rituals.
- **Magical Recipes and Crafts**: Learn to create delicious dishes, meaningful gifts, and enchanting décor, all infused with your loving intentions.

The Power of Intention

At the heart of every ritual is intention—the focused energy we direct toward a specific goal or desire. When you set an intention for your Valentine's Day rituals, you shift your celebration from routine to meaningful. Whether your goal is to reignite passion, express gratitude, or simply bask in the joy of love, your intention becomes the guiding light for your actions.

By combining intention with ritual, you open the door to transformation. You create space for love to grow, for wounds to heal, and for relationships to flourish. This book is your guide to harnessing that transformative power, using the magic of Valentine's Day to bring more love into your life.

A Day for Everyone

Valentine's Day is often seen as a holiday for couples, but the truth is that love belongs to everyone. Whether you're single, in a relationship, or somewhere in between, this guide is designed to help you celebrate the love in your life in all its forms. After all, the magic of Valentine's Day isn't limited to romance—it's about the universal energy of love that connects us all.

Your Journey Begins

As you turn the pages of this guide, remember that the most important ingredient in any ritual is your own heart. Approach each practice with an open mind and a loving spirit, and you'll find that the magic of Valentine's Day extends far beyond February 14th. By infusing love and intention into your actions, you create ripples of positivity that can transform your relationships, your perspective, and your life.

Welcome to a journey of love, magic, and meaning. Together, let's make this Valentine's Day one to cherish and remember.

Chapter 1: Setting Intentions for Love

In the realm of magic and manifestation, intention is everything. It is the seed from which all meaningful change grows. Setting clear, heartfelt intentions is the foundation for creating the love-filled life you desire. Whether you seek to deepen an existing relationship, call in new romance, or simply cultivate self-love, the act of setting intentions allows you to align your energy with your heart's desires.

This chapter will guide you through the process of setting powerful intentions for love, helping you understand the importance of clarity, focus, and emotional resonance in your practice. By the end of this chapter, you'll have the tools to craft meaningful intentions that serve as the cornerstone for the rituals and exercises to follow.

The Power of Intention

Intention is more than a wish; it is a deliberate and focused declaration of what you want to manifest. Unlike fleeting thoughts or vague desires, an intention carries the weight of your energy, commitment, and belief. It bridges the gap between thought and action, turning abstract ideas into tangible outcomes.

When it comes to love, setting intentions allows you to clarify your needs, align with your values, and communicate your desires to the universe. Love is a powerful energy, but it thrives when directed with purpose. By setting intentions, you create a beacon that attracts the experiences, people, and emotions that resonate with your heart.

What Makes a Strong Intention?

A strong intention is clear, specific, and rooted in authenticity. It should reflect your deepest truths and be free from fear, doubt, or societal expectations. Here are the key elements of a powerful intention:

1. **Clarity**: Vague intentions lead to vague outcomes. Instead of saying, "I want love," try, "I want a relationship built on mutual respect, trust, and emotional intimacy."
2. **Positivity**: Frame your intention in positive terms, focusing on what you want rather than what you wish to avoid. For example, say, "I attract a loving and supportive partner," rather than, "I don't want to be lonely."
3. **Emotion**: Infuse your intention with heartfelt emotion. Feel the joy, gratitude, and love as though your intention has already manifested. This emotional resonance amplifies your energy and signals to the universe that you're ready to receive.
4. **Authenticity**: Your intention should reflect your true self and values, not what others expect of you. Be honest about your desires and needs.
5. **Action-Oriented**: Intentions are most effective when paired with action. Consider how you can embody your intention in your daily life.

The Role of Self-Reflection

Before setting your intentions, it's essential to engage in self-reflection. Take time to explore your desires, beliefs, and patterns around love. Ask yourself:

- What does love mean to me?
- What do I value most in a relationship?
- What fears or limiting beliefs might be blocking me from experiencing the love I desire?
- How do I express love, and how do I prefer to receive it?

These questions help you uncover the underlying motivations and potential obstacles that shape your relationship with love. Journaling, meditating, or simply sitting in quiet contemplation can provide valuable insights that inform your intentions.

Crafting Your Love Intentions

Here's a step-by-step guide to crafting your love intentions:

1. **Create a Sacred Space**: Find a quiet, comfortable place where you can focus without distractions. Light a candle, play soothing music, or use crystals like rose quartz to enhance the energy of love.
2. **Visualize Your Desire**: Close your eyes and imagine the love you wish to experience. Picture the emotions, scenarios, and connections that bring you joy. The more vivid your visualization, the stronger your intention.
3. **Write It Down**: Use clear, concise language to articulate your intention. For example: "I intend to nurture a loving and harmonious relationship with my partner, built on trust, laughter, and mutual growth."

4. **State It in the Present Tense**: Frame your intention as though it is already happening. This creates a sense of immediacy and aligns your energy with your desired outcome.
5. **Feel the Emotion**: As you write or speak your intention, focus on the emotions it evokes. Feel the warmth, joy, and love as if your intention has already come to fruition.
6. **Commit to Your Intention**: Seal your intention with a simple affirmation, such as, "And so it is," or "This or something better, for the highest good of all."

Ritual for Setting Love Intentions

Here is a simple yet powerful ritual to set your love intentions:

Materials Needed:

- A journal or sheet of paper
- A pink or red candle (symbolizing love and passion)
- Rose quartz or another love-enhancing crystal
- Lavender or rose essential oil (optional)
- Matches or a lighter

Steps:

1. **Prepare Your Space**: Cleanse your space by smudging with sage or burning incense. Arrange your materials on a small altar or table.
2. **Ground Yourself**: Sit comfortably and take a few deep breaths. Close your eyes and feel your body relax as you connect with the energy of love.
3. **Anoint Your Candle**: If using essential oil, gently anoint the candle with the oil, moving in circular motions as you focus on your intention.

4. **Light the Candle**: As you light the candle, say aloud: "I light this flame as a beacon of love, to guide my intentions and illuminate my path."
5. **Write Your Intention**: Write your love intention in your journal or on a piece of paper. Be specific, positive, and heartfelt.
6. **Meditate on Your Intention**: Hold the paper and visualize your intention coming to life. Imagine yourself surrounded by the energy of love and joy.
7. **Seal the Ritual**: Place the paper under the candle or beside it. Say: "This intention is set with love and trust, carried to the universe to manifest in its perfect time."
8. **Let the Candle Burn**: Allow the candle to burn for as long as you feel is right (never leave it unattended). Extinguish it with gratitude when done.

Living Your Intention

Once your intention is set, embody it in your daily life. If you've set an intention to attract a loving partner, focus on being a loving and supportive person yourself. If your goal is to deepen an existing relationship, take steps to nurture connection and communication with your partner. By aligning your actions with your intention, you create the conditions for love to flourish.

Conclusion

Setting intentions is a powerful first step in transforming your relationship with love. It allows you to align your energy, clarify your desires, and create a roadmap for the loving connections you wish to cultivate. As you proceed through this guide, let your intentions serve as a guiding light, inspiring you to approach each ritual, practice, and moment with purpose and heart.

Love begins with intention—and with intention, anything is possible.

Chapter 2: Creating a Romantic Altar

In the world of magic and spiritual practices, altars serve as sacred spaces where energy, intention, and ritual converge. A romantic altar is a physical and energetic focal point for cultivating love, passion, and intimacy in your life. It acts as a visual and spiritual reminder of your intentions for love, whether they are self-directed, shared with a partner, or meant to draw love into your life.

In this chapter, you'll learn how to design, personalize, and maintain a romantic altar that reflects your unique desires and intentions. By the end, you'll have a beautiful, intentional space imbued with the energy of love and romance, ready to support your rituals and deepen your connection to this powerful energy.

The Purpose of a Romantic Altar

An altar is more than just a decorative arrangement—it is a sacred space where your energy and intentions are amplified. A romantic altar serves several purposes:

1. **Focus Your Intentions**: It provides a tangible place to focus your energy and clarify your desires for love and romance.
2. **Manifestation Tool**: By infusing the altar with your intentions, you create a magnet for love to flow into your life.
3. **Daily Reminder**: The altar acts as a physical reminder of your commitment to nurturing love in all its forms.
4. **Energetic Anchor**: It anchors love energy in your home, creating an atmosphere of warmth, passion, and connection.

Choosing the Right Location

Selecting the ideal location for your romantic altar is crucial, as it sets the tone for the energy you wish to cultivate. Here are some considerations:

- **Privacy**: Choose a location where you can engage with the altar without distractions. A bedroom, personal sanctuary, or a quiet corner in your home works well.
- **Energy Flow**: Avoid placing the altar in high-traffic areas or spaces with chaotic energy, such as near the television or work desk.
- **Alignment with Love Energy**: According to Feng Shui, the southwest corner of your space is associated with love and relationships, making it an excellent spot for a romantic altar.

Gathering Materials for Your Altar

A romantic altar can be as simple or elaborate as you wish. The key is to include items that resonate with your intentions and evoke feelings of love. Below is a list of common elements to consider:

1. Base or Surface

- A small table, shelf, or flat surface to serve as the foundation.
- Cover the surface with a cloth in romantic colors, such as red, pink, or white.

2. Candles

- Candles represent passion, warmth, and the fire of love.
- Use red or pink candles for romance and passion, white for purity and spiritual love, or gold for enduring connections.
- Place them in elegant holders to enhance the aesthetic.

3. Crystals

- Crystals amplify the energy of love and bring specific qualities to your altar:
    - **Rose Quartz**: The stone of unconditional love.
    - **Carnelian**: Enhances passion and sensuality.
    - **Amethyst**: Promotes emotional healing and spiritual connection.
    - **Garnet**: Symbolizes commitment and devotion.

4. Flowers and Plants

- Fresh flowers, such as roses, symbolize love, beauty, and romance.
- Jasmine, orchids, or tulips also carry loving energy.
- Potted plants like lavender or basil can add a grounding element to the altar.

5. Personal Tokens

- Items that hold sentimental value, such as a love letter, photograph, or jewelry.
- A symbolic item representing your ideal relationship, such as a figurine of two doves or intertwined hearts.

6. Symbols of Love

- Statues or images of deities associated with love, such as Aphrodite, Venus, or Cupid.
- Symbols like hearts, infinity signs, or the yin-yang to represent balance in love.

7. Aromatherapy

- Scent is a powerful tool for creating a romantic atmosphere.
- Use incense, essential oils, or sachets with scents like rose, vanilla, ylang-ylang, or patchouli.

8. Other Magical Tools

- A small dish or bowl for offerings, such as honey, chocolate, or wine.
- A journal or notebook to record your love intentions or experiences.
- Tarot cards or oracle cards focused on love themes.

Assembling Your Romantic Altar

Once you've gathered your materials, it's time to assemble your altar. Follow these steps to create a harmonious and energetically aligned space:

Step 1: Cleanse the Space

- Before setting up your altar, cleanse the area to remove stagnant or negative energy.
- Use sage, palo santo, or sound (e.g., ringing a bell) to purify the space.

Step 2: Arrange Your Items

- Begin with the foundational pieces, such as the cloth and candles.
- Place the crystals, flowers, and personal tokens in a visually pleasing arrangement.
- Ensure that everything feels balanced and intentional.

Step 3: Infuse Your Intentions

- As you place each item, focus on its purpose and the energy it brings to the altar.
- Speak your intentions aloud or silently, infusing the altar with your desires.

Step 4: Add a Centerpiece

- A centerpiece, such as a large rose quartz crystal or a statue of a love deity, can act as the focal point of the altar.

Step 5: Light It Up

- Light the candles and/or incense to activate the energy of the altar. Allow the flame and scent to carry your intentions into the universe.

Maintaining Your Romantic Altar

To keep your altar energetically vibrant and aligned with your intentions, regular maintenance is essential. Here are some tips:

1. **Cleanse Regularly**: Periodically cleanse the altar with sage, sound, or sunlight to refresh its energy.
2. **Change Items Seasonally**: Update flowers, candles, and decorations to reflect the changing seasons or your evolving intentions.
3. **Engage Daily**: Spend a few moments each day at your altar, meditating, journaling, or simply reflecting on love.
4. **Renew Offerings**: Replace food, drink, or other perishable offerings regularly to maintain a sense of freshness.

Using Your Romantic Altar

Your altar is a dynamic space that evolves with your journey. Here are some ways to use it:

- **Daily Reflection**: Begin or end each day by lighting a candle and reflecting on your intentions for love.
- **Rituals and Spells**: Use the altar as the focal point for romantic rituals, such as drawing love into your life or strengthening an existing relationship.
- **Celebration of Love**: Decorate the altar for special occasions like Valentine's Day or anniversaries, using it as a space to honor love in your life.
- **Visualization**: Meditate in front of your altar, visualizing your ideal relationship or love energy radiating from it.

Conclusion

Creating a romantic altar is an act of love in itself. It's a physical manifestation of your intentions, a sacred space where you can nurture your relationship with love. Whether you use it for daily reflection, magical rituals, or as a visual reminder of your desires, your altar will become a source of inspiration, comfort, and transformation.

Let your romantic altar be a testament to the power of love and intention, a space where magic and romance come alive in your everyday life.

Chapter 3: Love Spells and Affirmations

Love spells and affirmations have been used for centuries as tools to channel energy and manifest romantic, self-love, or relational goals. These practices empower you to align your intentions with the natural flow of the universe, amplifying the energy needed to attract and sustain love. In this chapter, we will explore the art of crafting and performing love spells, as well as the transformative power of affirmations.

Whether you are seeking new romance, strengthening an existing relationship, or nurturing your own self-love, this chapter will provide you with practical guidance and detailed instructions for using spells and affirmations to infuse your life with the magic of love.

The Essence of Love Spells

A love spell is an intentional ritual designed to focus your energy and align it with your desired outcome. Far from the stereotypical portrayals in popular media, love spells are not about manipulating others or forcing outcomes. Instead, they work by amplifying your own energy and intentions, creating the conditions for love to flourish naturally.

Key Principles of Love Spells

1. **Ethical Intentions**: Spells should always come from a place of love, respect, and authenticity. Avoid spells aimed at controlling or coercing others.
2. **Clear Intentions**: Be specific about what you desire. A vague intention will yield vague results.
3. **Focus on Yourself**: The most effective love spells often focus on enhancing your own capacity to give and receive love.
4. **Energy Alignment**: Your thoughts, emotions, and actions should align with the energy of love for the spell to manifest effectively.
5. **Letting Go**: After casting a spell, trust the universe and release your attachment to the outcome. This creates space for the energy to work.

Preparing for Love Spells

Before casting a love spell, take the time to prepare both your physical and energetic space. Proper preparation ensures that your energy is focused and your intentions are clear.

Cleansing Your Space

- Use sage, palo santo, or incense to remove stagnant or negative energy.
- Light a candle or use crystals to purify the space and invite positive energy.

Centering Yourself

- Meditate for a few moments to calm your mind and focus your energy.
- Visualize your desired outcome, allowing yourself to feel the emotions associated with your intention.

Gathering Materials

- Collect any materials required for your spell, such as candles, herbs, crystals, or personal tokens.
- Ensure your materials are chosen with intention, as each item carries symbolic energy.

Simple Love Spells

Below are some beginner-friendly love spells designed to attract love, enhance self-love, or strengthen an existing relationship.

1. Attracting New Love: The Rose Petal Spell
Materials Needed:

- A pink or red candle
- Rose petals (fresh or dried)
- Rose quartz crystal
- A piece of paper and pen

Steps:

1. Light the candle and place the rose quartz next to it.
2. Write your intention for love on the piece of paper (e.g., "I attract a loving, respectful, and joyful partner into my life").
3. Sprinkle rose petals around the candle in a circle, symbolizing the energy of love surrounding you.
4. Hold the paper and rose quartz in your hands. Visualize yourself surrounded by love and happiness.
5. Say aloud: "With an open heart, I welcome love into my life. Love flows to me freely, joyfully, and abundantly."
6. Place the paper under the candle and let the candle burn for a while. Extinguish it when you feel ready.
7. Keep the rose quartz with you as a talisman.

2. Strengthening an Existing Relationship: The Unity Knot Spell

Materials Needed:

- Two ribbons or cords in complementary colors
- A small charm or token symbolizing your relationship
- A white candle

Steps:

1. Light the white candle to symbolize unity and harmony.
2. Hold the two ribbons together and visualize your bond with your partner growing stronger.
3. Begin braiding or tying the ribbons together, incorporating the charm or token as you go.
4. With each knot or braid, repeat affirmations such as, "Our love is strong, resilient, and full of joy."
5. Once the ribbon is fully braided, place it near your altar or in a special place that represents your relationship.

3. Enhancing Self-Love: The Mirror Spell
Materials Needed:

- A mirror
- A pink candle
- Lavender or rose essential oil

Steps:

1. Anoint the pink candle with the essential oil and light it.
2. Sit in front of the mirror and look into your own eyes.
3. Say aloud: "I honor and love myself exactly as I am. I am deserving of love, joy, and abundance."
4. Take a moment to list things you love about yourself, speaking them aloud.
5. Gaze into the mirror with compassion, allowing yourself to feel the love and admiration you deserve.
6. Extinguish the candle and repeat this ritual as needed.

The Power of Affirmations

Affirmations are positive, present-tense statements that help reprogram your subconscious mind. When used consistently, they can shift your mindset, raise your vibration, and align you with the energy of love.

How Affirmations Work

- **Repetition**: By repeating affirmations regularly, you replace negative or limiting beliefs with empowering ones.
- **Emotional Resonance**: The more you feel the truth of an affirmation, the more effective it becomes.
- **Focus**: Affirmations keep your attention on your desires rather than fears or doubts.

Love Affirmations for Every Need

Here are some affirmations tailored to different aspects of love:

For Attracting Love

- "I am a magnet for love and joy."
- "Love flows to me effortlessly and abundantly."
- "I attract a partner who cherishes and respects me."

For Strengthening Relationships

- "Our love grows deeper and stronger every day."
- "We communicate with kindness and understanding."
- "Our relationship is built on trust, respect, and joy."

For Self-Love

- "I am worthy of love, happiness, and success."
- "I love and accept myself unconditionally."
- "I radiate confidence, beauty, and love."

For Healing Heartbreak

- "I release the past and open my heart to new beginnings."
- "I am whole and complete on my own."
- "Every experience brings me closer to the love I deserve."

Incorporating Spells and Affirmations into Your Routine

Consistency is key to making love spells and affirmations effective. Here are some tips for incorporating them into your daily life:

- **Morning Ritual**: Begin your day with a simple affirmation or a short spell to set the tone.
- **Journaling**: Write your affirmations or spell intentions in a journal, reinforcing them with each entry.
- **Visualization**: Combine affirmations with visualization techniques for a more powerful practice.
- **Meditation**: Meditate on your intentions, repeating affirmations as a mantra.

Conclusion

Love spells and affirmations are potent tools for aligning your energy with the love you seek. Whether you're casting a spell to attract romance, strengthen a bond, or nurture self-love, or repeating affirmations to reframe your mindset, these practices empower you to take an active role in manifesting your desires. Remember, the most important ingredient in any spell or affirmation is your own heartfelt intention.

With love as your guide, you hold the power to create the relationships and connections you desire.

Chapter 4: Candlelight Rituals for Couples

Candlelight has long been associated with romance, intimacy, and spiritual energy. Its warm glow creates an atmosphere of connection, while the flickering flames serve as a reminder of the dynamic and transformative power of love. Candlelight rituals are a meaningful way for couples to strengthen their bond, deepen intimacy, and celebrate their relationship. These rituals can be as simple or elaborate as desired, but their essence lies in the shared intention of two people coming together in love and unity.

In this chapter, we'll explore the magic of candlelight rituals for couples, offering detailed guidance on how to perform them, the symbolism behind them, and ways to personalize them for your unique relationship.

Why Candlelight Rituals for Couples?

Candlelight rituals hold a special place in the realm of romantic magic because they combine sensory, symbolic, and spiritual elements to create powerful experiences. Here's why they are so effective:

1. **Symbolism of Fire**: Fire represents passion, transformation, and energy. Lighting a candle during a ritual signifies igniting or strengthening these qualities in your relationship.
2. **Focus on Intention**: Candlelight rituals encourage couples to pause, set intentions, and connect on a deeper level.
3. **Enhancing Atmosphere**: The soft glow of candles fosters a sense of intimacy and calm, creating the perfect environment for meaningful interaction.
4. **Shared Experience**: Engaging in a ritual together strengthens the emotional and spiritual connection between partners.

Preparing for Candlelight Rituals

Before performing a candlelight ritual, it's essential to prepare both your physical space and your emotional state. Here's how:

1. Cleansing the Space

- **Smudging**: Use sage, palo santo, or incense to clear away negative energy.
- **Sound Cleansing**: Ring a bell or use a singing bowl to purify the space.
- **Decluttering**: Remove unnecessary items to create a serene and inviting environment.

2. Setting the Mood

- Dim the lights to let the candlelight take center stage.
- Play soft, romantic music or nature sounds to enhance the atmosphere.
- Use aromatherapy, such as rose, vanilla, or sandalwood essential oils, to evoke feelings of love and relaxation.

3. Gathering Materials

You'll need:

- **Candles**: Choose colors that symbolize your intention (e.g., red for passion, pink for love, white for purity, or gold for longevity).
- **Candle Holders**: Ensure they are stable and safe to use during the ritual.
- **Decorative Items**: Rose petals, crystals, or small tokens of love can add a personal touch.
- **A Lighter or Matches**: Use a new match or lighter to symbolize a fresh start.

4. Setting Intentions

Before beginning the ritual, discuss and agree on your shared intention. This could be to strengthen your bond, express gratitude for each other, or reignite passion.

Candlelight Rituals for Couples

Below are detailed candlelight rituals designed for various aspects of a relationship. Choose the one that resonates most with your current needs or adapt it to suit your preferences.

1. The Unity Flame Ritual

Purpose: To symbolize and strengthen the unity and partnership between you and your partner.

Materials Needed:

- One large white candle (representing your shared relationship)
- Two smaller candles (representing each partner)
- Matches or a lighter

Steps:

1. **Preparation**: Place the large candle in the center of your space with the two smaller candles on either side.
2. **Set Intentions**: Sit together and hold hands. Discuss what the unity flame symbolizes for your relationship (e.g., trust, love, or shared goals).
3. **Light Individual Candles**: Each partner lights one of the smaller candles, saying: "This flame represents my light, love, and commitment."
4. **Light the Unity Flame Together**: Using your smaller candles, light the large candle together, saying: "Together, our love burns brighter, stronger, and more beautiful."
5. **Reflect and Connect**: Sit in the candlelight, hold hands, and share what you appreciate most about each other. Let the unity candle burn for a while as a symbol of your connection.

2. Passion Ignition Ritual

Purpose: To reignite passion and intimacy in your relationship.

Materials Needed:

- Red or orange candles (symbolizing passion and energy)
- Rose petals or cinnamon sticks (optional)
- A journal or paper and pen

Steps:

1. **Set the Scene**: Scatter rose petals or cinnamon sticks around the candles for added symbolism.
2. **Light the Candles**: Light the red or orange candles together, saying: "With these flames, we reignite the passion that fuels our love."
3. **Write Your Desires**: Each partner writes down what they desire in terms of passion and intimacy, sharing them aloud if comfortable.
4. **Burn the Paper (Optional)**: Safely burn the papers in the flame of the candles, symbolizing the release of old energy and the welcoming of new passion.
5. **Embrace Each Other**: End the ritual with a hug, kiss, or intimate moment, letting the flames serve as a backdrop to your rekindled connection.

3. Gratitude Glow Ritual

Purpose: To express gratitude and appreciation for your partner and relationship.

Materials Needed:

- Yellow or gold candles (symbolizing gratitude and joy)
- A small bowl of water or wine
- Tokens of gratitude (e.g., a gift, letter, or flower)

Steps:

1. **Create the Circle**: Arrange the candles in a circle around a small bowl of water or wine.
2. **Set the Intention**: Each partner states their intention to honor and appreciate the other.
3. **Share Gratitude**: Take turns lighting a candle and sharing something you are grateful for in your partner.
4. **Exchange Tokens**: Give your partner the token you brought, explaining its significance.
5. **Seal the Ritual**: Clink glasses, take a sip of the water or wine, and say: "May our love continue to grow in gratitude and joy."

4. Renewal of Vows Ritual

Purpose: To reaffirm your commitment and love for each other.

Materials Needed:

- Two white candles and one red candle
- A small piece of paper with your vows written on it
- A ribbon or string (optional)

Steps:

1. **Light the Candles**: Light the two white candles, representing each partner's individuality.
2. **Read Your Vows**: Take turns reading your vows to each other, whether they are the original vows or new ones you've written.
3. **Light the Red Candle**: Together, use your individual candles to light the red candle, symbolizing your renewed commitment.
4. **Bind with Ribbon**: If desired, use a ribbon to gently tie your hands together as a symbol of your unity.
5. **Extinguish the White Candles**: Let the red candle burn as you extinguish the white candles, symbolizing the blending of your energies.

Tips for Personalizing Candlelight Rituals

- **Incorporate Personal Symbols**: Use items that hold sentimental value, such as wedding rings, photos, or shared mementos.
- **Include Favorite Scents**: Choose candles or incense with scents that evoke positive memories or feelings.
- **Adapt to Your Beliefs**: Modify rituals to align with your spiritual or cultural practices.
- **Keep It Intimate**: The most meaningful rituals are those that feel natural and personal to you as a couple.

Maintaining the Energy of the Ritual

After performing a candlelight ritual, it's important to carry the energy into your daily life:

- **Keep a Reminder**: Place the candles or items used in the ritual somewhere visible as a reminder of your intentions.
- **Practice Daily Acts of Love**: Use small, consistent gestures to reaffirm the energy created during the ritual.
- **Revisit the Ritual**: Repeat the ritual periodically to refresh and deepen its impact.

Conclusion

Candlelight rituals for couples are a beautiful way to celebrate love, intimacy, and connection. Through these rituals, you can honor your relationship, create lasting memories, and infuse your partnership with intention and magic. By embracing the power of candlelight, you invite warmth, passion, and harmony into your shared journey, illuminating the path toward deeper love and understanding.

Chapter 5: Self-Love Rituals for Singles

Self-love is the foundation of all other forms of love. It's the act of embracing yourself fully—your strengths, vulnerabilities, and everything in between. For singles, cultivating self-love is particularly vital, as it creates a strong sense of self-worth and independence, empowering you to attract healthier relationships and lead a more fulfilling life.

This chapter explores the transformative practice of self-love rituals, offering detailed guidance on how to honor and nurture yourself. These rituals are not just for healing or self-improvement but are acts of celebration, affirming your inherent value and unique beauty.

The Importance of Self-Love

Before delving into rituals, it's essential to understand why self-love is so powerful. Self-love isn't about arrogance or self-centeredness; it's about cultivating a healthy relationship with yourself. Here's why it matters:

1. **Emotional Resilience**: Self-love helps you navigate challenges with grace, as you draw strength from your inner foundation.
2. **Healthy Boundaries**: It empowers you to set boundaries and prioritize your well-being.
3. **Attracting Healthy Relationships**: When you love yourself, you naturally attract relationships that reflect that energy.
4. **Joyful Independence**: Self-love allows you to find fulfillment within, freeing you from dependency on external validation.

Preparing for Self-Love Rituals

To ensure your rituals are effective and meaningful, proper preparation is key. This involves creating the right physical and emotional space for your practice.

1. Cleansing Your Space

- **Smudging**: Use sage, palo santo, or incense to clear away negative energy.
- **Decluttering**: Remove any clutter to create an environment that feels calm and welcoming.

2. Setting the Mood

- Dim the lights or use soft, warm lighting.
- Play soothing music or nature sounds to create a relaxing atmosphere.
- Use scents like lavender, vanilla, or rose to evoke feelings of comfort and love.

3. Assembling Tools

Gather items that resonate with your intention, such as:

- Candles (pink for self-love, white for purity)
- Crystals (rose quartz, amethyst, or clear quartz)
- A journal or notebook
- Fresh flowers or plants
- Essential oils
- A mirror for reflection exercises

Self-Love Rituals

Below are detailed self-love rituals designed to enhance your sense of worth, nurture your inner being, and celebrate your individuality.

1. The Mirror Ritual

Purpose: To build confidence and foster self-acceptance by affirming your worth.

Materials Needed:

- A mirror
- A pink candle
- Rose essential oil (optional)

Steps:

1. **Set the Scene**: Light the pink candle and place it near the mirror. Anoint yourself with rose oil if desired.
2. **Gaze into Your Eyes**: Sit comfortably in front of the mirror and look into your own eyes.
3. **Speak Affirmations**: Say affirmations aloud, such as:
    - "I am worthy of love and respect."
    - "I embrace my uniqueness."
    - "I am enough just as I am."
4. **Express Gratitude**: Thank yourself for all you've done to overcome challenges and grow.
5. **Seal the Ritual**: Extinguish the candle with gratitude, and repeat this practice as often as needed.

2. The Bath of Radiance

Purpose: To cleanse negativity and recharge with loving energy.
Materials Needed:

- Epsom salts or Himalayan pink salt
- Rose petals or lavender
- Essential oils (rose, ylang-ylang, or chamomile)
- Candles

Steps:

1. **Prepare the Bath**: Fill your tub with warm water. Add salts, petals, and a few drops of essential oil.
2. **Set Your Intention**: Light candles around the bathroom and state your intention, such as, "I release negativity and invite love and light into my being."
3. **Immerse Yourself**: Soak in the water, visualizing it washing away self-doubt and filling you with confidence and love.
4. **Reflect**: Use this time to meditate or silently reflect on what you appreciate about yourself.
5. **End with Gratitude**: As you drain the tub, imagine negativity flowing away, leaving only radiant energy behind.

3. The Gratitude Ritual

Purpose: To shift focus from self-criticism to self-appreciation.

Materials Needed:

- A journal
- A pen
- A candle

Steps:

1. **Set the Mood**: Light a candle and sit in a quiet, comfortable space.
2. **Write Down Gratitudes**: List things you appreciate about yourself. Be specific, focusing on traits, actions, and qualities.
3. **Speak Them Aloud**: Read your list aloud, feeling the truth of each statement.
4. **Reflect**: Spend a few moments reflecting on how these qualities enhance your life.
5. **Close with Affirmations**: Say a closing affirmation, such as, "I am grateful for who I am and all I bring to the world."

4. The Self-Love Vision Board

Purpose: To visualize and manifest your highest version of self-love.

Materials Needed:

- A poster board or corkboard
- Magazines, photos, or printed images
- Scissors and glue
- Markers or pens

Steps:

1. **Gather Materials**: Collect images and words that inspire self-love and reflect your ideal life.
2. **Set Your Intention**: Before starting, state your intention, such as, "I create this vision to honor my journey of self-love."
3. **Assemble the Board**: Arrange and glue the images and words onto the board in a way that feels meaningful.
4. **Place It Somewhere Visible**: Keep the board in a place where you'll see it daily as a reminder of your self-love journey.

5. The Daily Ritual of Self-Care

Purpose: To integrate small, intentional acts of self-love into your daily routine.

Steps:

1. **Morning Check-In**: Begin your day with a self-love affirmation, such as, "Today, I honor my needs and nurture myself with love."
2. **Midday Pause**: Take a few moments to reflect on how you're feeling and make adjustments to meet your needs.
3. **Evening Reflection**: End your day with gratitude by writing down three things you appreciated about yourself or your day.

Crystals and Affirmations for Self-Love

Incorporating crystals and affirmations into your rituals can amplify their effects. Here are some recommendations:

Crystals

- **Rose Quartz**: The ultimate stone of unconditional love.
- **Amethyst**: Encourages self-awareness and emotional balance.
- **Citrine**: Promotes self-confidence and positivity.

Affirmations

- "I am my greatest source of love and joy."
- "I am deserving of all the good things life has to offer."
- "I release self-doubt and embrace my worth."

Maintaining the Energy of Self-Love

Rituals are a powerful start, but self-love requires consistent practice. Here's how to sustain the energy:

- **Daily Affirmations**: Repeat affirmations to reinforce your self-worth.
- **Celebrate Milestones**: Acknowledge your growth and achievements, no matter how small.
- **Practice Forgiveness**: Be gentle with yourself when mistakes happen, and treat setbacks as opportunities to grow.
- **Surround Yourself with Positivity**: Cultivate environments and relationships that support your self-love journey.

Conclusion

Self-love rituals for singles are acts of empowerment, helping you recognize your inherent value and embrace your uniqueness. By integrating these practices into your life, you nurture a deep, unshakable sense of self-worth that radiates outward, enriching every aspect of your existence. Remember, the most important relationship you'll ever have is the one with yourself—so make it a loving and magical one.

Appendix A: Tools and Resources for Romantic Rituals

Creating meaningful romantic rituals requires tools and resources that align with your intentions and resonate with your unique style. Whether you are a beginner exploring rituals for the first time or an experienced practitioner, the following comprehensive list of tools and resources will help you prepare, personalize, and enhance your rituals for love, passion, and connection.

1. Candles

Candles are essential for creating ambiance and focusing energy during rituals. The color, scent, and size of the candle can amplify your intentions.

Types of Candles:

- **Taper Candles**: Elegant and perfect for rituals focusing on long-term love and commitment.
- **Pillar Candles**: Symbolic of stability and strength in relationships.
- **Tealight Candles**: Ideal for simple, quick rituals or as part of a larger setup.
- **Chime Candles**: Small, fast-burning candles often used for focused intentions.

Candle Colors and Their Meanings:

- **Red**: Passion, desire, and physical intimacy.
- **Pink**: Unconditional love, romance, and emotional healing.
- **White**: Purity, unity, and spiritual love.
- **Gold**: Prosperity and long-lasting love.
- **Orange**: Joy and playful energy in relationships.

2. Crystals and Gemstones

Crystals carry specific energies that can enhance romantic rituals. They serve as focal points for intention setting and can be used in grids, meditations, or as altar decorations.

Crystals for Love:

- **Rose Quartz**: The ultimate stone of unconditional love and self-love.
- **Amethyst**: Promotes emotional healing and spiritual connection.
- **Garnet**: Symbolizes passion and commitment.
- **Rhodonite**: Heals past wounds and fosters forgiveness in relationships.
- **Clear Quartz**: Amplifies intentions and balances energies.
- **Carnelian**: Enhances sensuality and boosts confidence.

How to Use Crystals:

- Place them on your altar or around your candles.
- Hold them during meditations or visualizations.
- Create a crystal grid to amplify love intentions.

3. Essential Oils and Aromatherapy

Scents are powerful tools for evoking emotions and creating a romantic atmosphere. Essential oils can be used in diffusers, anointing candles, or blended into massage oils.

Recommended Essential Oils:

- **Rose**: Represents love, romance, and self-care.
- **Lavender**: Promotes relaxation and emotional balance.
- **Ylang-Ylang**: Enhances sensuality and deepens intimacy.
- **Jasmine**: Associated with passion and romance.
- **Sandalwood**: Grounds energy and fosters spiritual connection.

Applications:

- Add a few drops to a diffuser or oil burner to scent the space.
- Anoint candles, crystals, or your wrists before a ritual.
- Blend with carrier oils (e.g., coconut or almond oil) for romantic massages.

4. Altar Decorations

An altar serves as the focal point of your romantic rituals. Decorating it with intention creates a sacred and inspiring space.

Essential Altar Items:

- **Altar Cloths**: Use fabrics in romantic colors like pink, red, or white to cover the altar.
- **Flowers**: Roses, tulips, or jasmine to symbolize love and beauty.
- **Photographs or Tokens**: Personal items like a photo of you and your partner or a meaningful keepsake.
- **Symbols of Love**: Figurines, hearts, or infinity symbols to represent enduring affection.

- **Incense or Smudge Sticks**: Sage or palo santo to cleanse the space and invite positive energy.

5. Journals and Writing Tools

Writing is a powerful way to clarify intentions, reflect on emotions, and track progress in your love journey.

Uses in Rituals:

- Write love affirmations or gratitude lists.
- Document your intentions and experiences.
- Craft love letters to yourself or your partner.

Recommended Journals:

- A dedicated journal for love rituals, preferably in a color or design that resonates with your intentions.
- Blank notebooks or guided journals focused on love and relationships.

6. Divination Tools

Divination can provide insight into your love life and guide your intentions.

Common Tools:

- **Tarot Cards**: Look for love-themed spreads or use decks with romantic imagery.
- **Oracle Cards**: Choose cards that focus on relationships, self-love, or emotional healing.
- **Pendulums**: Use for yes/no questions about love or relationships.
- **Runes**: Explore rune meanings related to love, fertility, or harmony.

7. Music and Sound

Music enhances the atmosphere of rituals and helps set the emotional tone.

Recommended Types of Music:

- Instrumental music with soft, romantic tones.
- Nature sounds like gentle rain or ocean waves.
- Specific playlists for love and relaxation.

Sound Tools:

- Singing bowls to raise the vibration of your space.
- Chimes or bells to mark the beginning and end of rituals.

8. Herbs and Flowers

Herbs and flowers are natural allies in love rituals, representing growth, beauty, and vitality.

Popular Choices:

- **Rose Petals**: Universal symbol of love and romance.
- **Lavender**: Calms and balances emotions.
- **Basil**: Attracts love and commitment.
- **Cinnamon**: Adds warmth and passion.
- **Chamomile**: Promotes harmony and relaxation.

Uses in Rituals:

- Scatter them around your altar or in a ritual bath.
- Burn dried herbs as part of your ceremony.
- Include them in sachets or love charms.

9. Ritual Foods and Beverages

Incorporating symbolic foods and beverages can make rituals more immersive.

Suggestions:

- **Chocolate**: Represents sweetness and indulgence.
- **Honey**: Symbolizes the sweetness of love and attraction.
- **Wine or Juice**: Used in toasts or offerings to symbolize unity and celebration.

10. Resources for Inspiration

To deepen your knowledge and practice, explore these resources:

Books:

- *Love Magic: Over 250 Spells and Potions for Getting It, Keeping It, and Making It Last* by Lilith Dorsey.
- *The Crystal Bible* by Judy Hall (for crystal recommendations).
- *Romancing the Ordinary: A Year of Simple Splendor* by Sarah Ban Breathnach.

Websites and Communities:

- Online forums or social media groups dedicated to love rituals and magic.
- Websites offering free tarot spreads or guided meditations for love.

Workshops and Classes:

- Local or virtual workshops on candle magic, crystal healing, or aromatherapy.
- Online courses focused on self-love and relationship-building.

11. Storage and Maintenance Tools

Proper storage ensures your tools remain energetically and physically clean.

Suggestions:

- Velvet pouches or boxes for crystals and tarot cards.
- Airtight containers for herbs and flowers.
- A dedicated space to keep candles, journals, and other ritual supplies.

Conclusion

The tools and resources outlined in this appendix provide everything you need to create personalized and meaningful romantic rituals. By thoughtfully selecting and using these items, you can enhance your practice and bring deeper intention, beauty, and magic to your journey with love.

Message from the Author:

I hope you enjoyed this book, I love astrology and knew there was not a book such as this out on the shelf. I love metaphysical items as well. Please check out my other books:

-Life of Government Benefits

-My life of Hell

-My life with Hydrocephalus

-Red Sky

-World Domination:Woman's rule

-World Domination:Woman's Rule 2: The War

-Life and Banishment of Apophis: book 1

-The Kidney Friendly Diet

-The Ultimate Hemp Cookbook

-Creating a Dispensary(legally)

-Cleanliness throughout life: the importance of showering from childhood to adulthood.

-Strong Roots: The Risks of Overcoddling children

-Hemp Horoscopes: Cosmic Insights and Earthly Healing

- Celestial Hemp Navigating the Zodiac: Through the Green Cosmos

-Astrological Hemp: Aligning The Stars with Earth's Ancient Herb

-The Astrological Guide to Hemp: Stars, Signs, and Sacred Leaves

-Green Growth: Innovative Marketing Strategies for your Hemp Products and Dispensary

-Cosmic Cannabis

-Astrological Munchies

-Henry The Hemp

-Zodiacal Roots: The Astrological Soul Of Hemp

- **Green Constellations: Intersection of Hemp and Zodiac**

-Hemp in The Houses: An astrological Adventure Through The Cannabis Galaxy

-Galactic Ganja Guide

Heavenly Hemp

Zodiac Leaves
Doctor Who Astrology
Cannastrology
Stellar Satvias and Cosmic Indicas
<u>Celestial Cannabis: A Zodiac Journey</u>
AstroHerbology: The Sky and The Soil: Volume 1
AstroHerbology:Celestial Cannabis:Volume 2
Cosmic Cannabis Cultivation
The Starry Guide to Herbal Harmony: Volume 1
The Starry Guide to Herbal Harmony: Cannabis Universe: Volume 2
Yugioh Astrology: Astrological Guide to Deck, Duels and more
Nightmare Mansion: Echoes of The Abyss
Nightmare Mansion 2: Legacy of Shadows
Nightmare Mansion 3: Shadows of the Forgotten
Nightmare Mansion 4: Echoes of the Damned
The Life and Banishment of Apophis: Book 2
Nightmare Mansion: Halls of Despair
<u>Healing with Herb: Cannabis and Hydrocephalus</u>
Planetary Pot: Aligning with Astrological Herbs: Volume 1
Fast Track to Freedom: 30 Days to Financial Independence Using AI, Assets, and Agile Hustles
<u>**Cosmic Hemp Pathways**</u>
How to Become Financially Free in 30 Days: 10,000 Paths to Prosperity
Zodiacal Herbage: Astrological Insights: Volume 1
Nightmare Mansion: Whispers in the Walls
The Daleks Invade Atlantis
Henry the hemp and Hydrocephalus

10X The Kidney Friendly Diet
Cannabis Universe: Adult coloring book
Hemp Astrology: The Healing Power of the Stars

Zodiacal Herbage: Astrological Insights: Cannabis Universe: Volume 2

Planetary Pot: Aligning with Astrological Herbs: Cannabis Universes; Volume 2

Doctor Who Meets the Replicators and SG-1: The Ultimate Battle for Survival

Nightmare Mansion: Curse of the Blood Moon

The Celestial Stoner: A Guide to the Zodiac

Cosmic Pleasures: Sex Toy Astrology for Every Sign

Hydrocephalus Astrology: Navigating the Stars and Healing Waters

Lapis and the Mischievous Chocolate Bar

Celestial Positions: Sexual Astrology for Every Sign

Apophis's Shadow Work Journal: : A Journey of Self-Discovery and Healing

Kinky Cosmos: Sexual Kink Astrology for Every Sign

Digital Cosmos: The Astrological Digimon Compendium

Stellar Seeds: The Cosmic Guide to Growing with Astrology

Apophis's Daily Gratitude Journal

Cat Astrology: Feline Mysteries of the Cosmos

The Cosmic Kama Sutra: An Astrological Guide to Sexual Positions

Unleash Your Potential: A Guided Journal Powered by AI Insights

Whispers of the Enchanted Grove

Cosmic Pleasures: An Astrological Guide to Sexual Kinks

369, 12 Manifestation Journal

Whisper of the nocturne journal(blank journal for writing or drawing)

The Boogey Book

Locked In Reflection: A Chastity Journey Through Locktober
Generating Wealth Quickly:
How to Generate $100,000 in 24 Hours
Star Magic: Harness the Power of the Universe
The Flatulence Chronicles: A Fart Journal for Self-Discovery
The Doctor and The Death Moth
Seize the Day: A Personal Seizure Tracking Journal
The Ultimate Boogeyman Safari: A Journey into the Boogie World and Beyond

Whispers of Samhain: 1,000 Spells of Love, Luck, and Lunar Magic: Samhain Spell Book

Apophis's guides:

Witch's Spellbook Crafting Guide for Halloween

Frost & Flame: The Enchanted Yule Grimoire of 1000 Winter Spells

The Ultimate Boogey Goo Guide & Spooky Activities for Halloween Fun

Harmony of the Scales: A Libra's Spellcraft for Balance and Beauty
The Enchanted Advent: 36 Days of Christmas Wonders

Nightmare Mansion: The Labyrinth of Screams

Harvest of Enchantment: 1,000 Spells of Gratitude, Love, and Fortune for Thanksgiving

The Boogey Chronicles: A Journal of Nightly Encounters and Shadowy Secrets

The 12 Days of Financial Freedom: A Step-by-Step Christmas Countdown to Transform Your Finances

Sigil of the Eternal Spiral Blank Journal

A Christmas Feast: Timeless Recipes for Every Meal

Holiday Stress-Free Solutions: A Survival Guide to Thriving During the Festive Season

Yu-Gi-Oh! Holiday Gifting Mastery: The Ultimate Guide for Fans and Newcomers Alike

Holiday Harmony: A Hydrocephalus Survival Guide for the Festive Season

Celestial Craft: The Witch's Almanac for 2025 – A Cosmic Guide to Manifestations, Moons, and Mystical Events

Doctor Who: The Toymaker's Winter Wonderland

Tulsa King Unveiled: A Thrilling Guide to Stallone's Mafia Masterpiece

Pendulum Craft: A Complete Guide to Crafting and Using Personalized Divination Tools

Nightmare Mansion: Santa's Eternal Eve

Starlight Noel: A Cosmic Journey through Christmas Mysteries

The Dark Architect: Unlocking the Blueprint of Existence

Surviving the Embrace: The Ultimate Guide to Encounters with The Hugging Molly

The Enchanted Codex: Secrets of the Craft for Witches, Wiccans, and Pagans

Harvest of Gratitude: A Complete Thanksgiving Guide

Yuletide Essentials: A Complete Guide to an Authentic and Magical Christmas

Celestial Smokes: A Cosmic Guide to Cigars and Astrology

Living in Balance: A Comprehensive Survival Guide to Thriving with Diabetes Insipidus

Cosmic Symbiosis: The Venom Zodiac Chronicles

The Cursed Paw of Ambition

Cosmic Symbiosis: The Astrological Venom Journal

Celestial Wonders Unfold: A Stargazer's Guide to the Cosmos (2024-2029)

The Ultimate Black Friday Prepper's Guide: Mastering Shopping Strategies and Savings

Cosmic Sales: The Astrological Guide to Black Friday Shopping

Legends of the Corn Mother and Other Harvest Myths

Whispers of the Harvest: The Corn Mother's Journal

The Evergreen Spellbook

The Doctor Meets the Boogeyman
The White Witch of Rose Hall's SpellBook
The Gingerbread Golem's Shadow: A Study in Sweet Darkness
The Gingerbread Golem Codex: An Academic Exploration of Sweet Myths
The Gingerbread Golem Grimoire: Sweet Magicks and Spells for the Festive Witch
The Curse of the Gingerbread Golem
10-minute Christmas Crafts for kids
Christmas Crisis Solutions: The Ultimate Last-Minute Survival Guide
Gingerbread Golem Recipes: Holiday Treats with a Magical Twist
The Infinite Key: Unlocking Mystical Secrets of the Ages
Enchanted Yule: A Wiccan and Pagan Guide to a Magical and Memorable Season
Dinosaurs of Power: Unlocking Ancient Magick
Astro-Dinos: The Cosmic Guide to Prehistoric Wisdom
Gallifrey's Yule Logs: A Festive Doctor Who Cookbook
The Dino Grimoire: Secrets of Prehistoric Magick
The Gift They Never Knew They Needed
The Gingerbread Golem's Culinary Alchemy: Enchanting Recipes for a Sweetly Dark Feast
A Time Lord Christmas: Holiday Adventures with the Doctor
Krampusproofing Your Home: Defensive Strategies for Yule
Silent Frights: A Collection of Christmas Creepypastas to Chill Your Bones
Santa Raptor's Jolly Carnage: A Dino-Claus Christmas Tale
Prehistoric Palettes: A Dino Wicca Coloring Journey
The Christmas Wishkeeper Chronicles
The Starlight Sleigh: A Holiday Journey
Elf Secrets: The True Magic of the North Pole
Candy Cane Conjurations
Cooking with Kids: Recipes Under 20 Minutes

Doctor Who: The TARDIS Confiscation
The Anxiety First Aid Kit: Quick Tools to Calm Your Mind
Frosty Whispers: A Winter's Tale
The Infinite Key: Unlocking the Secrets to Prosperity, Resilience, and Purpose
The Grasping Void: Why You'll Regret This Purchase
Astrology for Busy Bees: Star Signs Simplified
The Instant Focus Formula: Cut Through the Noise
The Secret Language of Colors: Unlocking the Emotional Codes
Sacred Fossil Chronicles: Blank Journal
The Christmas Cottage Miracle
Feeding Frenzy: Graboid-Inspired Recipes
Manifest in Minutes: The Quick Law of Attraction Guide
The Symbiote Chronicles: Doctor Who's Venomous Journey
Think Tiny, Grow Big: The Minimalist Mindset
The Energy Key: Unlocking Limitless Motivation
New Year, New Magic: Manifesting Your Best Year Yet
Unstoppable You: Mastering Confidence in Minutes
Infinite Energy: The Secret to Never Feeling Drained
Lightning Focus: Mastering the Art of Productivity in a Distracted World
Saturnalia Manifestation Magick: A Guide to Unlocking Abundance During the Solstice
Graboids and Garland: The Ultimate Tremors-Themed Christmas Guide
12 Nights of Holiday Magic
The Power of Pause: 60-Second Mindfulness Practices
The Quick Reset: How to Reclaim Your Life After Burnout
The Shadow Eater: A Tale of Despair and Survival
The Micro-Mastery Method: Transform Your Skills in Just Minutes a Day
Reclaiming Time: How to Live More by Doing Less
Chronovore: The Eternal Nexus

The Mind Reset: Unlocking Your Inner Peace in a Chaotic World
Confidence Code: Building Unshakable Self-Belief
Baby the Vampire Terrier
Baby the Vampire Terrier's Christmas Adventure
Celestial Streams: The Content Creator's Astrology Manual
The Wealth Whisperer: Unlocking Abundance with Everyday Actions
The Energy Equation: Maximize Your Output Without Burning Out
The Happiness Algorithm: Science-Backed Steps to Joyful Living
Stress-Free Success: Achieving Goals Without Anxiety
Mindful Wealth: The New Blueprint for Financial Freedom
The Festive Flavors of New Year: A Culinary Celebration
The Master's Gambit: Keys of Eternal Power
Shadowed Secrets: Groundhog Day Mysteries
Beneath the Burrow: Lessons from the Groundhog
Spring's Whispers: The Groundhog's Prediction
The Limitless Mindset: Unlock Your Untapped Potential
The Focus Funnel: How to Cut Through Chaos and Get Results
Bold Moves: Building Courage to Live on Your Terms
The Daily Shift: Simple Practices for Lasting Transformation
The Quarter-Life Reset: Thriving in Your 20s and 30s
The Art of Shadowplay: Building Your Own Personal Myth
The Eternal Loop: Finding Purpose in Repetition
Burrowing Wisdom: Life Lessons from the Groundhog
Shadow Work: A Groundhog Day Perspective
Love in Bloom: 5-Minute Romantic Gestures
The Shadowspell Codex: Secrets of Forbidden Magick
The Burnout Cure: Finding Balance in a Busy World
The Groundhog Prophecy: Unlocking Seasonal Secrets
Nog Tales: The Spirited History of Eggnog
Six More Weeks: Embracing Seasonal Transitions
The Lumivian Chronicles: Fragments of the Fifth Dimension

Money on Your Mind: A Beginner's Guide to Wealth
The Focus Fix: Breaking Through Distraction
January's Spirit Keepers: Mystical Protectors of the Cold
Creativity Unchained: Unlocking Your Wildest Ideas in 2025
Manifestation Mastery: 365 Days to Rewrite Your Reality
The Groundhog's Mirror: Reflecting on Change
The Weeping Angels' Christmas Curse
Burrowed in Time: A Groundhog Day Journey
Heartbeats: Poems to Share with Your Valentine
Dino Wicca: The Sacred Grimoire of Prehistoric Magick
Courage of the Pride: Finding Your Inner Roar
The Lion's Leap: Bold Moves for Big Results
Healthy Hustle: Achieving Without Overworking
Practical Manifesting: Turning Dreams into Reality in 2025
Jurassic Pharaohs: Unlocking the Magick of Ancient Egypt and Dino Wicca
The Happiness Equation: Small Changes for Big Joy
The Confidence Compass: Finding Your Inner Strength
Whispers in the Hollow: Tales of the Forgotten Beasts
Echoes from the Hollow: The Return of Forgotten Beasts
The Hollow Ascendant: The Rise of the Forgotten Beasts
The Relationship Reset: Building Better Connections
Mastering the Morning: How to Win the Day Before 8 AM
The Shadow's Dance: Groundhog Day Symbolism
Cupid's Kitchen: Quick Valentine's Day Recipes
Valentine's Day on a Budget: Love Without Breaking the Bank
Astrocraft: Aligning the Stars in the World of Minecraft
Forecasting Life: Groundhog Day Reflections
Bleeding Hearts: Twisted Tales of Valentine's Terror
Herbal Smoke Revolution: The Ultimate Guide to Nature's Cigarette Alternative
Winter's Wrath: The Complete Survival Blueprint for Extreme Freezes.

The Groundhog's Shadow: A Tale of Seasons
Burrowed Insights: Wisdom from the Groundhog
Sensual Strings: The Art of Erotic Bondage
Whispered Flames: Unlocking the Power of Fire Play
Forgotten Shadows: A Guide to Cryptids Lost to Time
Six Weeks of Secrets: Groundhog Day's Hidden Messages
Shadows and Cycles: Groundhog Day Reflections
The Art of Love Letters: Crafting the Perfect Message
Romantic Getaways at Home: Turning Your Space into Paradise
Purrfect Brews: A Cat Lover's Guide to Coffee and Companionship
The Groundhog's Wisdom: Timeless Lessons for Modern Life
The Shadow Oracle: Groundhog Day as a Predictor
Emerging from the Burrow: A Journey of Renewal
The Language of Love: Learning Your Partner's Love Style
Authorpreneur: The Ultimate Blueprint for Writing, Publishing, and Thriving as an Author
Weathering the Seasons: Groundhog Day Perspectives

If you want solar for your home go here: https://www.harborsolar.live/apophisenterprises/

Get Some Tarot cards: https://www.makeplayingcards.com/sell/apophis-occult-shop

Get some shirts: https://www.bonfire.com/store/apophis-shirt-emporium/

Instagrams:
@apophis_enterprises,
@apophisbookemporium,
@apophisscardshop
Twitter: @apophisenterpr1
Tiktok:@apophisenterprise
Youtube: @sg1fan23477, @FiresideRetreatKingdom
Hive: @sg1fan23477
CheeLee: @SG1fan23477

Podcast: Apophis Chat Zone: https://open.spotify.com/show/5zXbrCLEV2xzCp8ybrfHsk?si=fb4d4fdbdce44dec

Newsletter: https://apophiss-newsletter-27c897.beehiiv.com/

If you want to support me or see posts of other projects that I have come over to: **buymeacoffee.com/mpetchinskg**

I post there daily several times a day

Get your Dinowicca or Christmas themed digital products, especially Santa Raptor songs and other musics. Here: **https://sg1fan23477.gumroad.com**

Apophis Yuletide Digital has not only digital Christmas items, but it will have all things with Dinowicca as well as other Digital products.

Festival Fun Activity Book

Shivasree Bhowmik

Ukiyoto Publishing

All global publishing rights are held by

Ukiyoto Publishing
Published in 2021

Content Copyright © **Shivasree Bhowmik**

ISBN 9789364945790

All rights reserved.
No part of this publication may be reproduced, transmitted, or stored in a retrieval system, in any form by any means, electronic, mechanical, photocopying, recording or otherwise, without the prior permission of the publisher.

The moral rights of the author have been asserted.
This is a work of fiction. Names, characters, businesses, places, events, locales, and incidents are either the products of the author's imagination or used in a fictitious manner. Any resemblance to actual persons, living or dead, or actual events is purely coincidental.

This book is sold subject to the condition that it shall not by way of trade or otherwise, be lent, resold, hired out or otherwise circulated, without the publisher's prior consent, in any form of binding or cover other than that in which it is published.

www.ukiyoto.com

Hola!

Mother Goddess Durga, our Goddess of Strength, is coming in town to protect us from all danger and gift us prosperity, peace and happiness.

Colour and know some amazing facts about our beloved Mother Goddess and fuel our brainpower.

Amazing Fact-1
She is the divine mother of all creation, a protector and a warrior

Amazing Fact-2
She is a powerful goddess who can vanquish demons single-handedly

Amazing Fact-3
She is the mother who devotes herself to her four children

Amazing Fact-4
She stands for supreme strength, courage, love, and care

Amazing Fact-5
The trinity of Brahma, Vishnu and Shiva together created her - the Mother of the Universe - who ensures creation, preservation and destruction of all evil forces

Dot2Dot

Join the Dots to see what's ten-armed Goddess holding in her arms and learn their symbolic meanings!

Amazing Fact-6
Chakra: Gifted by Lord Vishnu
Symbolizes: Cycle of our life which keeps us moving

Amazing Fact-7
Lotus: Gifted by Lord Brahma
Symbolizes: Awakening of our wisdom and attainment through knowledge

Amazing Fact-8
Sword: Gifted by Lord Ganesha
Symbolizes: Sharpness of our intellect that helps us to make right choices over wrong

Amazing Fact-10
Conch: Gifted by Lord Varuna
Symbolizes: 'AUM' sound which has the power to destroy all the negative energies

Amazing Fact-9
Trishul: Gifted by Lord Shiva
Symbolizes: Its three points mean past, present and future and the centre spike means our awareness

Dot2Dot

Join the Dots to see what's in the other 4 arms of our ten-armed Goddess and learn their symbolic meanings!

Amazing Fact-11
Bow and arrow: Gifted by Lords Vayu and Surya
Symbolizes: Our focus on our duties, clarity of our dreams and our potential to attain our goals independently

Amazing Fact-12
Axe: Gifted by Vishwakarma
Symbolizes: We need to kill all our negative feelings

Amazing Fact-13
Vajra/Thunderbolt: Gifted by Lord Indra
Symbolizes: Our strong character, determination and supreme power which will resolve our problems in life without losing our confidence

Page - 3

Avatars of Goddess Durga

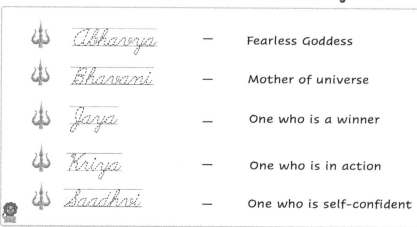

Devi Durga has many Avatars (superpowers). Find different Avatar names by tracing over dotted lines and know their meanings too.

⚔ *Abhaya*	—	Fearless Goddess
⚔ *Bhavani*	—	Mother of universe
⚔ *Jaya*	—	One who is a winner
⚔ *Kriya*	—	One who is in action
⚔ *Saadhvi*	—	One who is self-confident

Which talent (superpower) do u have?

Draw your own avatar as a SuperDancer or SuperSinger or Super-Mathematician or anything you are good at.

Doodle Dhak
(An Indian Drum)

Learn an amazing fact about Dhak and have fun coloring bright and beautiful Dhak! 😊

Amazing Fact-15

Dhak: **This drum beats calls you to celebrate the joy of victory**

Nine colors of Navratri

This festival celebrates Goddess Durga for defeating the demon Mahishasura in a battle that lasted for 9 nights. Nav means Nine and Ratri means night, thus its name. It celebrates the victory of good over evil. These nine days are dedicated to Durga and her nine avatars - the Navadurga. There is also 9 colors of Navratri for each day depicting nine incarnations of Goddess.

Colour each flower petal as numbered in the factfiles and learn what each color means. 😊

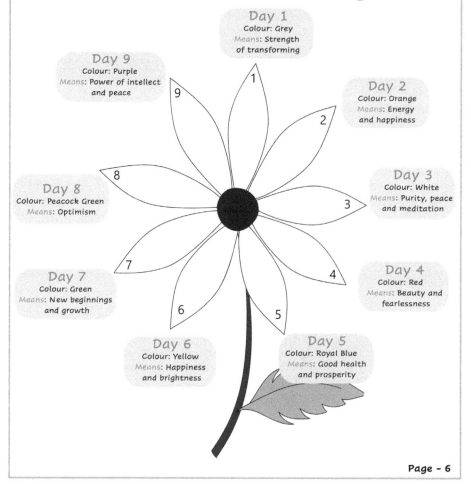

Day 1
Colour: Grey
Means: Strength of transforming

Day 2
Colour: Orange
Means: Energy and happiness

Day 3
Colour: White
Means: Purity, peace and meditation

Day 4
Colour: Red
Means: Beauty and fearlessness

Day 5
Colour: Royal Blue
Means: Good health and prosperity

Day 6
Colour: Yellow
Means: Happiness and brightness

Day 7
Colour: Green
Means: New beginnings and growth

Day 8
Colour: Peacock Green
Means: Optimism

Day 9
Colour: Purple
Means: Power of intellect and peace

Doodle Ghat

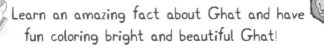

Learn an amazing fact about Ghat and have fun coloring bright and beautiful Ghat!

Amazing Fact-15

Ghat sthapana is the most important ritual of puja. It happens on the first day of Navratri and is taken care of through the nine-day festival. It is the incarnation of Goddess Durga!

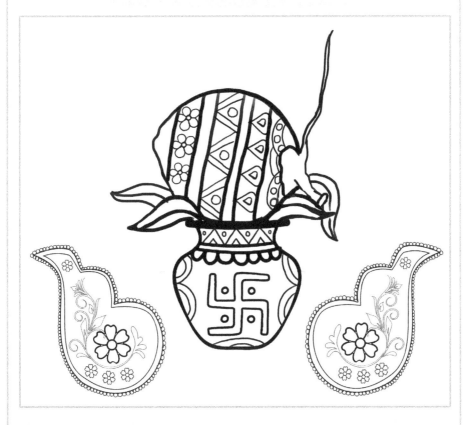

Memory Game : Find all the amazing facts in this book and check how many you can remember

Navratri Map of India

Our beautiful, diverse, colorful India as different states celebrate the auspicious 10 days festival period of Autumn in different ways.

Observe the map of India and trace with color pencils the different greetings from different states of India as they celebrate this festival in different ways!

Amazing Fact-16

Ayudhya Puja: This is celebrated in many parts of South India on the ninth day where tools, books, musical instruments, machinery and automobiles are worshipped along with the worship of Goddess Saraswati

How to draw a Lion?

Learn the 5 easy steps to draw a Lion. 😊

Draw your LION, take a pic and post it on Brainpower Books FB page
(https://www.facebook.com/Brainpower-Books-102125861916742) **as**
#BrainpowerBooksLion

Durga Puja Wordsearch

Find all the magical words of this celebration!

See how many of these words you can find in the letters below. The words may be written across, up, down, diagonally and even backwards.

P	F	D	E	V	I	D	S	A	T
P	R	O	T	E	C	T	O	R	J
p	I	O	a	l	t	B	A	D	H
B	L	S	B	L	A	N	K	I	T
l	D	H	S	G	a	U	T	T	G
J	F	U	N	W	H	B	I	K	N
A	G	B	U	B	O	T	P	A	E
Y	J	H	I	a	V	R	O	H	R
A	O	O	F	R	L	O	D	S	T
P	I	Y	G	C	W	O	R	B	S
S	H	A	R	A	D	I	Y	A	J
T	E	G	A	R	U	O	C	Y	B

SHUBHO SHAKTI PROTECTOR COURAGE POWER
BIJAYA SHARADIYA DEVI SWORD STRENGTH

Page - 10

Pandal Hunt

There are so many Puja pandals. We all visit pandals in and around our neighbourhood.

Find four Puja pandals in and around your neighbourhood.

Dussehra Crossword

Use the clues to complete the crossword puzzle and have fun using your brainpower! 😊

Across:
1. Which flower is Goddess holding?
2. Ravana was killed by whom?
3. Which weapon is used to kill the demon?
4. On which animal is she riding?
5. Dussehra is celebrated on the T...... day of Navaratri

Down:
1. How many children does Goddess have?
2. In which season this festival is celebrated?
3. How many hands does Goddess have?
4. Who is Rama's wife?
5. How many eyes does Goddess have?

Dussehra - VijayaDashami

Dussehra is a festival celebrated across North India, to celebrate Lord Ram's triumphant victory over Lankan King Raavan after he kidnapped his wife, Sita. This festival marks the tenth day of Navaratri.

Learn 2 facts about VijayaDashami and color the below image using your creative colouring skills

Amazing Fact-17
The fight to save Goddess Sita lasted for 10 days. Lord Ram defeated Ravana with the help of Divyastra given by Goddess Durga

Amazing Fact-18
The day when Lord Ram killed Ravana was the Dashami, the tenth day of Ashwin (Autumn) month and hence it is called Vijaya Dashami

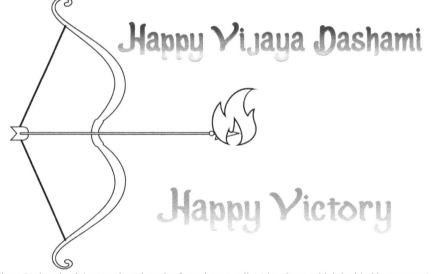

Vijaya Dashami celebrates the triumph of good over evil. Write down which bad habit you want to give up and which good habits/talents of yours you want to focus and practice so you can become a super hero.

_____

_____

P.S. Remember Bow and arrow symbolizes our focus on our duties, clarity of our dreams and our potential to attain our goals independently

Navratri Greetings Card

Color your own card and cut it to gift your loved ones.

Amazing Fact-16

Dandiya: A traditional dance between women and men, also known as **sword dance** as it shows a mock battle between Goddess Durga and the demon

Wishing you all very Happy Navratri!

Spot the difference

Spot 12 differences in the images below.

Hunt Game : : Eye Spy with your little eyes how many Lions can you find hidden in these pages? Hunt and count them down here _____

Hello Autumn!

Goddess Durga is worshipped in Autumn (Sharad) season. In Sanskrit, Sharad means Autumn!

What can you see in Autumn? Match sentences on left with pictures on right.

Amazing Fact-16
Autumn season is from mid September to mid November

- 🍁 Leaves changes to yellow/orange/brown

- 🍁 Falling leaves

- 🍁 Kans grass (Kash phool)

- 🍁 Misty mornings

- 🍁 Migrating birds

- 🍁 Pine cone starts appearing

- 🍁 Conkers start appearing

- 🍁 Weather becomes cooler

- 🍁 Shorter days/longer nights

- 🍁 Calendar months September/October/November

Page - 16

Navratri Story

Goddess Durga symbolizes strength and courage. This 9 - day festival is a wonderful opportunity for us to do amazing acts of strength and courage!

Write a story where you have shown the virtues of courage and strength by helping someone in need or helping your friends, parents or siblings. You may write what amazing activities you did with your family and friends together. 😍

My Navratri/Durgatsav Story

Hola!

Lets celebrate Ganesh Chaturthi!

Lord Ganehsa is coming in town to gift us wisdom, success and remove all our obstacles to help us start new beginnings!!

Lets learn some amazing facts about our Lord to fuel our brainpower.

Colour and know our beloved Lord!

Amazing Fact-1
He is the God of New Beginnings, Success and Wisdom

Amazing Fact-2
Lord Ganehsa has a sweet tooth

Amazing Fact-3
He is the remover of Obstacles

Amazing Fact-4
He is a mouse riding God

Amazing Fact-5
He has an elephant head

Dot2Dot

Join the Dots to know and learn the symbolic items in Lord Ganesha's hands!

Amazing Fact-6
Axe symbolizes remover of all obstacles

Amazing Fact-7
Lotus symbolizes awareness

Amazing Fact-8
Laddoo – sweet which he is very fond of

Names of Lord Ganesha

Lord Ganesha is known by many names which are derived from Sanskrit language.

Find the different names by tracing over the dotted lines and know their meanings too.

- *Avighna* — One who takes away all problems and pain
- *Amit* — Incomparable Lord
- *Bhalchandra* — One who carries the moon on his head
- *Bhupati* — Lord of the Gods
- *Ekdant* — One who has the face of an elephant but has only one tusk, hence he is also called Ekdant
- *Sumukh* — One with an auspicious face
- *Tarun* — One who is ageless
- *Vinayaka* — God of wisdom

Now, write your name in Cursive: _____

What does your name mean? _____

Do you have other names, like a nickname? _____

If yes, write your other names _____

Ganesh Chaturthi

This festival celebrates the arrival of Ganesha on earth from Kailash Parvat with his mother Goddess Parvati.

Color the picture using your creative skills and imagination!

Amazing Fact-9
Ganesh Chaturthi is celebrated for 10 days

Amazing Fact-10
The festival ends on tenth day, when idol is carried in a public procession with music and group chanting then immersed in a nearby waterbody

How to draw Ganesha from Om?

Learn all the 5 easy steps to draw Lord Ganesha.

Draw your Ganesha, take a pic and post it on Brainpower Books FB page
(https://www.facebook.com/Brainpower-Books-102125861916742) *as*
#BrainpowerBooksGanesha

Shop Puja Items

Lets go shopping to buy all the essential puja items. The kids look at the shelf and points the items to the shopkeeper.

Circle all the puja items on the shelf and match them with the list.

1) Panchapradip   2) Diya   3) Dhoop   4) Bells
5) Flowers   6) Garland   7) Ganga Jal   8) Chandan
9) Sweets   10) Shankha

Doodle Om

Learn amazing fact about sound Om and have fun coloring a bright and beautiful Om!

Amazing Fact-11

"OM" symbolizes the Universe. It is the most important Hindu symbols. It represents three aspects of God: the Brahma, the Vishu and the Shiva.

Memory Game

Find all the amazing facts in this book and check how many you can remember! 😎

Page - 24

Ganesh Chaturthi Crossword

Use the clues from fact files to complete the crossword puzzle and have fun using your brainpower! 😊

Across:
1. Who is the brother of Lord Ganesha?
2. Lord Ganesha is the God of W.....
3. What is he riding on?
4. He has an E....... head.
5. For how many days Ganesh Chaturthi is celebrated?

Down:
1. Who is the mother of Lord Ganesha?
2. He is fond of S....
3. Who is the father of Lord Ganesha?
4. He removes all O.....
5. What is he holding in one of his upper arms?

Spot the difference

Spot 12 differences in the images below.

Hunt Game : I spy with my little eyes, find the rat hidden in every page and see how many you can find _____

Ganesh Chaturthi Wordsearch

Find all the magical words of this celebration!

See how many of these words you can find in the letters below. The words may be written across, up, down, diagonally and even backwards.

A	B	U	B	E	G	I	N	N
B	A	K	H	J	Y	U	I	O
A	W	A	R	E	N	E	S	S
K	R	Z	X	C	B	R	P	T
K	I	G	A	N	A	P	A	T
A	O	B	Y	N	G	H	V	F
I	L	B	F	S	G	H	J	L
L	M	U	G	P	R	J	K	M
A	B	D	M	Q	U	T	Y	C
S	F	D	N	L	K	N	I	X
H	D	H	F	O	J	J	E	S
E	E	I	D	V	U	B	O	A
R	W	R	S	B	G	F	O	Q
W	Q	A	K	A	Y	A	N	I

Awareness Beginning Pune Ganapati Vinayaka
Buddhi Chaturthi Kailash Siddhi Idol

Laddoo and Modak Game

Delicious modaks (sweet dumplings) are Lord Ganesha's most favourite sweets. He is also called Modakpriya for his great love for modak.

Lord Ganesha is also very fond of ladoos.

1.

Draw a circle around half? How many laddoos have you circled?

_____

2.

Draw a circle around half? How many Modaks have you circled?

_____

3.

Draw a circle around half? How many laddoos have you circled?

_____

4.

Draw a circle around half? How many Modaks have you circled?

_____

Challenge – How many modaks are in ¼th of group 2?
How many modaks are in ¼th of group 4?

Ganesh Chaturthi Laddoo Hunt

Lord Ganesha loves Laddoos. We all love Laddoos. Especially the Besan Laddoos.!

Lets find them hidden in these tricky mazes. Oh what fun these hunts are!!

Letter to my Lord Ganesha

Lets write an open letter to him seeking blessings of Wisdom and Knowledge. Let Lord helps us remove all the obstacles and helps us start a great new beginning! 😍

My dear Lord Ganesha,

I love you. I tried my best to do all my homeworks on time.

Hola!
Its Lord **Krishna's** Birthday!!

Lets learn some amazing facts about our Lord to fuel our brainpower.
Colour and know our beloved Lord!

Amazing Fact-1
He is the god of protection, compassion, tenderness, and love

Amazing Fact-2
He is worshipped as the eighth avatar of Vishnu and also as the supreme god

Amazing Fact-3
Krishna's birthday is celebrated every year by Hindus on Krishna Janmashtami which falls in late August or early September

Amazing Fact-4
He is the central character in Bhagavad Gita

Amazing Fact-5
The name "Krishna" originates from the sanskrit word KRSNA, Which means "Dark Blue" or "The All Attractive"

Dot2Dot

Join the Dots to know some more amazing facts about Little Krishna, called Gopal!

"Hare Krishna Hare Krishna, Krishna Krishna Hare Hare,
Hare Rama Hare Rama, Rama Rama Hare Hare"

Amazing Fact-6
The divine child Krishna is known as Bal Gopal

Amazing Fact-7
As a child, Gopal was a prankster which earn him the nickname Makhan Chor (butter thief)

Amazing Fact-8
Gopal was also a protector and people in Gokul and Vrindavan loved him

Amazing Fact-9
Little Krishna lifts the Govardhan hill to protect the people of Vrindavan from devastating rains and floods

Amazing Fact-10
Go - pala means, One who protects anyone in journey of life completing the great circle! Go - round, Pala - protector

Names of Lord Krishna

Lord Krishna is known by many names in different states of India.

Find the different names by tracing over the dotted lines.

- *Kanhaiya* — in Uttar Pradesh
- *Jagannath* — in Odisha
- *Vithoba* — in Maharashtra
- *Shrinathji* — in Rajasthan
- *Guruvayorappan* — in Kerala
- *Dwarakadheesh* — in Gujarat
- *Parthasarathy* — in Tamil Nadu

Amazing Fact-11
Jagannath means Lord of the universe

Amazing Fact-12
Keev is another name of Lord Krishna. Its named after mother Devaki and father Vasudeva and is used for child form of Krishna

Amazing Fact-13
Lord Krishna's sister is Subhadra and brother is Balaram

Now, write your name in Cursive: _____

What does your name mean? _____

How to draw and color a peacock feather?

Learn all the easy steps to draw your peacock feather in just 8 easy steps

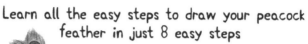

Amazing Fact-14
A peacock feather is thought of as a symbol of goodluck in most parts of the world!!

Memory Game : Find all the amazing facts in this book and check how many you can remember!

Janmashtami Crossword

Use the clues from the factfiles to complete the crossword puzzle and have fun using your brainpower 😊

Across:
1. What is Lord Krishna known as in Odissa?
2. What is baby Krishna called?
3. Where was Lord Krishna Born?
4. Name Lord Krishna's sister
5. What is he holding in his hands?

Down:
1. Who gave birth to Lord Krishna?
2. Who raised Lord Krishna?
3. Name Lord Krishna's brother
4. What does baby Krishna love to eat?
5. Krishna's crown is made of P....... feather

Spot the difference

Use your curious eyes to spot 12 differences in each set of images below and have fun! 😊

Janmashthami Wordsearch

Find all the magical words of this celebration!
See how many of these words you can find in the letters below. The words may be written across, up, down, diagonally and even backwards.

```
V I V D E V A K I
T R A Z T U L E M
P E I W G B C T A
K Q U N K Q U U K
R W D Y D P D L K
I G I T A A E F H
S R A T U D V V A
H A D I T G A A N
N D V A S U D F N
A H L O R D N L U
S A J Y A M U N A
U D L U K O G T E
```

| VRINDAVAN | KRISHNA | RADHA | LORD |
| GITA | FLUTE | MAKKHAN | GOKUL | YAMUNA |

Dahi Handi game

Krishna Janmashthami is celebrated in variant ways in different parts of India. In Maharashtra, Dahi Handi (vessel of curd) is celebrated, where a group of young men make a tower and break the vessel.

Lets go shopping to find the perfect Handi. The kids look at the shelf where the handis were kept.

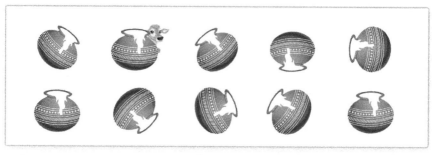

The shopkeeper turns some of the handis to show them properly. Which handis did not get flip?

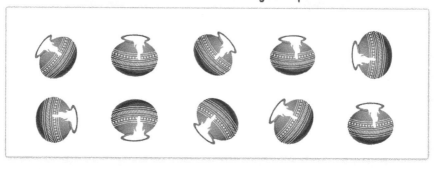

Which of these letters look the same after they've been flipped from side to side?

D P X W V G I T A

Peacock Feather Doodling

Doodle with Peacock feathers and have fun coloring them bright and beautiful!

Know season Monsoon!

Janmashthami is celebrated during rainy season known as Monsoon.
The word "monsoon" is from the Arabic word mausim meaning "season of winds".

Learn the signs of rainy season by matching sentences on left with pictures on right.

- Monsoon starts in the month of June and lasts until September

- July and August are the rainiest months

- Has very pleasant weather with cool breeze and rain showers

- Plants, trees, and grasses look very green

- Ponds, rivers, streams receive plenty of rainwater

- Environment becomes clean and fresh due to heavy shower

- Dark clouds and lightning occur

- Rainwater helps farmers for cultivation of crops

- Gives us different types of fruits and vegetables

Janmashthami Cheese Hunt

We all love cheese, butter, cream. Don't we?

Lets find them hidden in these tricky mazes.
Oh what fun these hunts are!! 😍

Janmasthami Greetings Card

Colour your own card and cut it to gift your loved ones.

Wishing you all very Happy Janmashtami!!!

May Lord Krishna give you all love, peace and happiness

Janmashthami Prasad

Learn what items make a Prasad and match the prasad labels on the right with the correct Prasad plates on the left.

Charnamrit is a sweet and milky concoction, which is offered to devotees as part of prasad. Its made by blending milk, yogurt, ghee, honey, Charnamrit is also used to bathe the feet of Lord Krishna's idol.

Makhan paag is made with lotus seeds, ghee, milk and sugar.

Kheer is made from rice, condensed milk, grated almonds and pistachios.

     Makhan paag

     Kheer

     Charnamrit

Hunt Game

I spy with my little eyes - Find the calf hidden in every page and see how many you can find

Janmashthami Diary

Krishna teaches us to live in present moment. Mindfulness is all about staying in present and NOT worry about the future.

Write your diary using some words from lists below.

Today is _____

Names, Place, Things
Home, school, neighbourhood, gifts, toys, sweets, prasad, bells, decorations, friends, parents, brother, sister, relatives, makkhan pot

Wow words
Beautiful, amazing, wonderful, lovely, busy, nice, shimmering, joyous, happy, kind

Action words
praying, worship, walk, jump, play, laugh, smile, cry, cook, make, share

Page - 44

Milton Keynes UK
Ingram Content Group UK Ltd.
UKHW042341121024
449589UK00001B/136